TOOTH GAPS IN THE ARCHIVES

TOOTH GAPS IN THE ARCHIVES

a record of the last dry-born

Poems by

Francis Dylan Waguespack

Button Publishing Inc.

Minneapolis

2026

TOOTH GAPS IN THE ARCHIVES
POETRY
AUTHOR: Francis Dylan Waguespack
COVER DESIGN: Coral Black

◇

◇

button poetry

Published by Button Poetry
Minneapolis, MN 55418 | http://www.buttonpoetry.com

◇

Manufactured in the United States of America
PRINT ISBN: 978-1-63834-150-5

First printing

This work is for anyone who knows what it feels like to live through the first days, first weeks, first years after The Storm. For the people of the Gulf Coast, but especially those touched by the 2005 Federal Floods, the 2016 Louisiana Floods, and Hurricane Ida in 2021. For the kids whose questions still haven't been answered.

For the dead, the missing, the heartbroken, the displaced. For the people of New Orleans.

This work is for us.

Oh Sweet Jesus the levees that break in my heart
— Frank Stanford

TABLE OF CONTENTS

TOOTH GAPS IN THE ARCHIVES

TOOTH GAPS IN THE ARCHIVES

Each lost record is a tooth wrenched free.
The clerk says, "Nothing's missing, it was just
never there," as I tongue the sockets of my history,
tasting rust where roots should grip.

"No name like that here."   *Absence, she thinks, is a tidy void.*

In the archives' gut, water scars cling to files
like plaque. Folders from the '27 flood
sprout black mold, pages fused, once-healthy
teeth the state carves out, expendable.

The archivist,   *gloved and masked, pries them loose.*

I stand barefaced, inhaling
that too familiar scent of what's gone.
Someone's everything, a curation snag,
deep in a cavity the state won't probe.

Cross-filed between parishes,   *loss hums the drill's song.*

Our bodies hoard what paper sheds.
Mémère slurs her sister's name,
gone from frames, from files,
a splinter lodged in the roof of her mouth.

I inherit it raw, a gap   *tender as a cracked root.*

In Plaquemines Parish, five cemeteries
have molted into the Gulf since '32,
plastic polyester flowers smothered
by smooth cordgrass and black rush, rising.

Call it nature's clerking   *but to me, it's a canal through marrow.*

The archivists shed whatever won't scan,
tag misfits "miscellaneous," leave mandibles
yawning in state-shined jars. "We're keeping
history for tomorrow," the manager boasts.

I ask, "Whose?" His smile,   *all teeth, doesn't reach his eyes.*

I hoard my own memories, stubborn
as a calcium deposit. I bury names on higher ground.
The state's memory picks its keepers, but my cells
encode what they extract. I'm a wisdom tooth:

inflamed, crooked, pressing   *sideways through their no.*

I tongue the sockets. I chart a map
the state can't shred. My voice becomes
a smuggler's code for dragging
the missing home. This is my rite:

to name the gaps,   *to bare them,*

to spit the numb   *of forgetting back.*

I.

BLACK RUSH RISING

No shelter, no home, no claim to dry land.
Some things   *float*
                                    sink.
But fire ants form a lethal life raft,
ready to swarm whatever they touch.

DO NOT RETURN HOME, CHILD.

The one you knew is long buried
under frigerator muck and Mississippi mud,
cypress knees kneelin over funeral plots where
the ground holds its dead like your mama holds her liquor.

All that remains is the waste tires
        and the flaking doubloons
        and the sun-bleached beads,

those wind chimes swingin   in the heavy breeze,
chemical rainbows where egrets once nested are puddles
no child should jump in.   *Do not return home, child.*

The Phone Company never got the lines back up, and the
    Gas Company never did pay out the lawsuits, and the
    City Council codifies empty promises in a empty chamber.

Do not return home, child.   Your daddy can't sing
your lullaby over that generator hum, and besides, he has
to work nights at the orange-glow refinery that replaced
your broken Ariel the Mermaid nightlight.

Here is the truth: You were born in a dying place,
and we knew before you got here you would live to see its end.

Come here, baby
girl, trade that white
altar server robe for one
of our long black ones
and meet us in the sacristy.

We've reserved your place
on the risers in our choir
of collective mourning.

Join us! in the intergenerational gnawing grief known
only by the ones who've paid enough attention
to know that the city been dying since the day
it was born, and that all empires eventually fall
from within, and that you children would pay
the debts we amassed when we bet y'all futures

and lost.
all the while, tellin
anybody who'd listen
it was all to give y'all
better, more than we had.

Do not return home, child.

Your Mr. Bingle, and your
Beanie Babies, and your
lovie blanket
have made good homes
for black mold, that slow,
quiet reclamation more honest
than any res tor at ion project
with its sand-pumpin promises.

It speaks a truth we just can't—some things will not be saved.

Do not return home, child. There is no home for you here.

There is no home for you.

08/28/2021 1400 / ORLEANS PARISH

24 hours til landfall: We drive through underpasses and lots, calling out. Alex, the street team leader, knows everybody by name. *The NOAA says it's gonna be bad. Cat 4, maybe 5*, we say. Some faces turn away, wordless. A few join us in the van. A man by the lakefront folds his tarp deliberately, says he'll take his chances with the storm before handing his humanity over to the shelter. We leave cards with a city phone number, knowing they'll be paper pulp by tomorrow.

It's just the two of us. Shelter workers are working at shelters and people who work in nonprofit offices are in air-conditioned hotel rooms three hundred miles inland. I learn the city pulled the port-a-potties from all the camps last week.

No shits given—just taken.

SUBSIDENCE

Millimeters (Annual Measurement)

In Terrebonne Parish, subsidence occurs at a rate
of thirty-five millimeters per year, a disappearance act
measured in a stretching distance between step and ground,
in water lines on buildings like faded magic-marker
charting growth spurts on your childhood bedroom door.

The Corps calls this *relative sea level rise*,
a bureaucrat's term for drowning.

Once, we believed that concrete could save us,
poured into foundations, formed into levees,
the illusion of permanence hardening into place.
But concrete itself subsides, cracks, tilts seaward.
Nothing we build escapes the physics of sinking.

What we call permanent could only ever be provisional
next to water's ancient patience.

Centimeters (Human Lifetime)

We adapt without noticing: the extra cement
poured each year to level porches, heirlooms
settling into new homes on higher shelves,
the casual way we say it's always flooded here
when history and soil samples say otherwise.

This slow normalization of loss
might be our most dangerous adaptation.

South of Golden Meadow, you can stand
where maps still show land, body impossibly
buoyant over ghosted properties, gulf rippling
over what tax records still list as residential lots.
Paperwork doesn't sink as fast as soil.

The land and the law might subside at different rates,
but neither can be trusted to hold you.

Meters (Generational Scale)

Your cousin adds cinderblocks to his hunting camp in Cocodrie
each season, a slow elevator rising from the edge of the earth.
He says it's easier than selling, says he's gaining elevation
while the world sinks around him. You admire his obstinance,
so you don't tell him it's no match against the river's hydrology.

We can't run from the compacting of sediment
cut from its source when we built the levees.

At the water's edge, oak tree skeletons stand in formation,
bone-white and leafless, a vanguard. They don't topple
dramatically as you might expect. They simply dissolve,
molecule by molecule, cellulose digested by salt and sun,
until one morning, you notice a tree is shorter.

Years later, you notice it's gone—you didn't have time
to watch the clock's hour hand move.

Kilometers (Historical Record)

Engineers avoid certain words: abandonment, retreat, loss.
They talk instead of adaptation strategies, resilience planning,
managed retirement of assets. Euphemisms echo in half-empty
town halls, language subsiding under the weight of denial,
attendance abating as residents relocate, as hope too subsides.

The scrape of folding chairs being put away grows
louder than the voices of those who remain.

Loss measured in millimeters feels manageable
until you multiply by decades, centuries, millennia.
Until your old grocery store, your mom's grammar school
become nautical navigation hazards, the roads on GPS
leading you straight into open water.

In Terrebonne Parish, subsidence occurs at a rate
of thirty-five millimeters per year.

In a lifetime, that's enough to drown a world.

JOHN MCPHEE

In a brutalist cube in Northwest DC,
we hunch over MacBooks
and seek the magic words to sway

America

not to hate
trans kids.

Outside, the Potomac flows
relentless
while we draft controlled language
to defend uncontrollable bodies.

I miss my home. I cannot help
but spend my days
evangelizing

my Louisiana.

A friend leans in one day, says
when I talk about the South,
I sound like John McPhee.

I tell her what he might.
That back home,
the river wants
its old course back.

And of how familiar this feels,
institutions constructing
elaborate systems
to force nature's movement
through unnatural channels.

I tell her, let us be the flood,
and let our bodies carve new
channels, levees be damned,
and we will flow homeward
by any route
we choose.

08/12/2016 1100 / IBERVILLE PARISH

Water follows the lowest path. The floodwaters found routes through our neighborhood I never knew existed—crawlspaces, concrete culverts, the minor depression where 74 meets Oak. The depth is added to by the police station across the street. They're pumping water from their parking lot into my driveway; it laps at my front door. The drainage ditch around my small farm has no obstructions, my neighbor Jimmy showed me how to clear it with diesel fire last week (you need a little gasoline to get it going). Jimmy can break me into my car with a fishing rod and a tube of paint. I wonder if he knows how to get this water out of here.

A FOOTBALL FIELD OF LAND LOST EVERY HOUR

the radio says,
which is more precise than I want to know
when I'm frying an egg at 6 AM.

A football field is my dad's whole childhood,
the tire swing, the crawfish pond,
the patch where his pépère grew mirlitons,
the spot where he hollered come get dinner,
the kitchen where three generations learned
that the difference between a good roux
and a burned one is thirty seconds
and your full attention.

But on the news, they say football field
and football fields we understand,
football fields are replaceable, you can
build one anywhere there's grass
and chalk. A football field every hour
sounds like something we could save
if we tried hard enough, if we cared
enough, sounds like losing nothing
we can't live without.

At 7 AM, gone is the dock where
Jean tied his pirogue in early mornings
'fore the sun came up, where he cleaned
his catch and threw the heads to pelicans,
who were always on time for
their breakfast.

By 8 AM, saltwater has claimed
the sweetest little fishing hole
in Vermillion Parish and the cabin
where the Thibodaux boys learned
to play bourré on summer nights
when the air was warm but
the breeze felt cool and nobody
wanted to go
inside.

At 9 AM, farewells are bid
to an ancient island with thirty names
that no more exists except in the minds
of the people who have to move inland and try
to explain to their kids what a fishing camp was,
what it meant to be from where the land met the gulf
in a slow dance that lasted ten thousand years
and spun out in only
one hundred.

At 10 AM, I finish my coffee and all of us lose
the hardwood swamp where 100 million monarchs
rest on their way south, one last stop,
just before the oil platforms, loses one more hour
of a place that was here long before we invented
football fields to measure its drowning,
grain by grain, yard by yard,
a football field of forever
every hour,
every hour.

08/29/2021 2200 / ORLEANS PARISH
16TH ANNIVERSARY OF HURRICANE KATRINA

Find something heavy, I tell her, phone chiming a warning in my ear, buttons my sweat is dialing. *An axe. A hammer. Anything heavy made of metal.* She puts me on speaker so she can search. Cabinets opening, drawers slamming. Her aunt murmurs something in the background. *Yes,* I say, get upstairs, *get to the attic now if the water's rising. Bring water and flashlights and batteries. But listen—*

How do you tell a child not from here, born only months before The Storm, of the writing on houses, *2 dead in attic* scrawled in blood red spray paint? Trapped between lumber and black water, abandoned by their country, victims of heat, thirst, and help that came too late. *You might need to make a hole. Through the roof. To get out.* The line cracks. I hear water. I hear fear. I hear her say they found a crowbar under the sink. Good girl. Smart girl. I tell her to call 911 again, keep calling, but also to take that crowbar to the attic. Just in case.

16 and 64 alone in a flooded house.
How many more calls before the lines shut off?

OUT PAST THE LEVEE DISTRICTS

The notice said: drainage complete
by Friday. The notice said: contamination
below concern. The mayor posed
with a borrowed mop. We put chairs
on the porch, lined our boots
by the door. We wanted to believe
it was over.

Joseph stopped draining the canoe
between storms. Ellie patched her tarp
with a window awning. Grams laminated
the insurance cancellation, pinned it up
with all her prayer cards collected
at funerals. We started boiling all the water
before the notices arrived.

We boxed the wedding china
in fish crates, sent our heirlooms
up the bayou to live
on firmer ground.

We stopped saying,
when the power's back on.
We stopped asking,
when are they coming to help?
Instead we asked,
what can we carry by raft?

One night, the kids chalked
the high-water line on the vinyl siding.
No one erased it come morning.

08/12/2016 1400 / IBERVILLE PARISH

A friend calls from Texas to say she heard on the news that everything is fine now, the flood's receding. I stand in water, thigh-deep and still rising, dog a lamb across my shoulders, scanning for cottonmouth snakes and fire ant islands, "everything's fine." She can't help here, and I can't take care of her feelings.

LIVING AUTOPSY REPORT: NEW ORLEANS, LOUISIANA

COORDINATES: 29.9511° N, 90.0715° W
TIME OF EXAMINATION: In progress (terminal prognosis)
MEASUREMENTS: 349.8 sq miles, 95% below sea level
POPULATION: 376,971 (down from pre-Katrina 484,674)

EXTERNAL EXAMINATION

Subject presents as urban center in Mississippi River
deltaic plain, bordered by Lake Pontchartrain (north),
Mississippi River (south/west), wetland remnants (east).

Bowl-shaped topography with severe subsidence evident.
External surface marked by grid-pattern scarring (streets),
with architectural stratification indicating repeated cycles
of construction, destruction, and rebuilding.

Evidence of historical trauma visible in infrastructure,
presenting as compromised arterial roads, collapsed
drainage systems, abandoned / destroyed public housing.

This does not account for the heat of a brass band
at full volume, for the way we all dance despite it all,
for the second line erupting on a Sunday afternoon,
transforming mourning into joy and grief into rhythm.

Visible defensive structures (levees, floodwalls,
pumping stations) show evidence of repeated failure
and reinforcement.

Close examination reveals engineering compromise:
built to protect commerce over communities, and designed
to channel water out of white neighborhoods into Black ones.

The pumping stations do still hum.
Men still stand knee-deep in water
with wrenches and prayers. Failure
is pending, just as it has for decades.

TOXICOLOGY

Contamination Assessment

Lead content: 6.5x EPA safety thresholds
Core samples: petrochemical saturation extending to water table
Subsidence rate: 2 inches per year in Lakeview and Gentilly
Cancer cluster hotspots: consistent with "Cancer Alley" industrial corridor
PFAS concentrations: rising, particularly in childcare centers and schools

Water samples reveal concerning levels of industrial contaminants from "Cancer Alley" industrial corridor upstream. Surface water contains:

Benzene: 5.2x allowable limits
Mercury: 3.9x allowable limits
Microplastics: 8,342 particles per liter

Hurricane Katrina floodwaters (2005) introduced:

E. coli (3.8x safe levels); **Petroleum products; Heavy metals; Mold spores** (Stachybotrys chartarum, Aspergillus)

We still drink the water. What else is there to do?
The tap's stream transports the memory of every
place it has seen, every body it has passed through,
every storm it's ever ridden, every story it has witnessed.
We drink our own history, contamination and all.

SYSTEMS ANALYSIS

Drainage System

Wooden water lines (circa 1900) still in use
Pumping stations operating beyond capacity
Multiple points of impending failure identified
Maintenance crews understaffed by 63%

The system resembles an aging heart attempting to circulate through clogged arteries, each rainfall a stress test inching it closer to catastrophic failure.

Hydrological System

Critical dysfunction in flood control mechanisms.
Natural drainage severed by canal construction.
Wetland buffer reduced by 50% since the 1930s.
Evidence of maladaptive intervention throughout,
prioritizing development over long-term stability.

Kids still splash in puddles after storms,
squealing as counterpoint to the anxious
calculations of parents watching the sky.

Cultural System

Examination reveals complex multicultural tissue,
areas of remarkable resilience alongside necrotic zones.
Post-K demographics: 31% reduction in Black population
Gentrification markers in Bywater, Tremé, Mid-City
Accelerated cultural extraction patterns; customs
and traditions treated as resources to be mined.

But the horns keep playing.
The dancers still take to the streets.
Every Sunday, somebody turns a corner
with a drum and people follow.
Even now, the metronome of the city's
heartbeat refuses to slow, even here,
as the waters rise around her.

Economic System

Tourism economy presents as parasitic relationship:
Housing costs: increased 84% since 2005
Median income: risen only 12% (adj. for inflation)
Wealth distribution: concentrated in corporate structures
Adjacent neighborhoods: poverty 2.4x national avg.
Service industry wages: insufficient for residents
to afford homes in the neighborhoods they maintain

A tourist drops twenty dollars on beignets. A musician plays for change. Somewhere in the Bywater, a developer buys another shotgun house, paints it pastel pink, and lists it on Airbnb. The transaction is complete: culture converts to commodity, history to experience, community to backdrop.

PROGNOSIS

Terminal condition confirmed. Current models
indicate subject will be 82% submerged by 2050
if global carbon emissions continue at present rates.

Evidence of multiple organ failure:

Infrastructure collapse imminent (7-10 years)
Affordable housing extinction (3-5 years)
Cultural displacement reaching critical threshold (ongoing)
Essential services interruption frequency increasing exponentially

People still come home, even when there is no home to return to. The city is dying, but she refuses to die quietly.

She insists on music until the very end.

NOTES AND OBSERVATIONS

I find myself unable to maintain clinical distance.
The subject still pulses with life, even as water rises around her.

My diagnostic equipment fails to measure what matters most:
the communal will to remain, the stubborn insistence on joy
despite all evidence suggesting despair would be more appropriate.

There's no way for me to capture the look of iron lace
in morning light, the smell of jasmine and satsuma blossoms
after rainfall, the arced sound of a brass band turning
a corner at dusk, the grip of a stranger's hand helping
you up, the taste of the first rainbow snowball of summer.

This city knows how to die. She has practiced
for 300 years. She understands that documentation
requires more than measurement, that some vital signs
cannot be quantified, only witnessed.

What I cannot determine is whether this time is different—
whether water has its own inevitable verdict that even she,
with her centuries of practice, cannot dance her way through.

In the distance, a child splashes through a flooded street,
laughing as water reaches her knees. She screams
and raises her arms, imitating the tuba player passing by,
smile and instrument both gleaming gold.

08/12/2016 1700 / IBERVILLE PARISH

Things that float:

plastic toys
protest flyers
picture albums
prescription bottles
three shoes (none matching)
my annotated copy of *As I Lay Dying*
the numbers 3 and 7 from my house address
a calico cat captaining a frigerator-turned-pirogue
rumors about somebody—anybody—who might be coming to help

ANOTHER HURRICANE POEM

typical morning orange juice orange yolks smear the
kitchen counter first drops hit like pennies then
nickels then harder something's tearing
loose next door stilts swaying toilet
spitting slipping on wet floor
wind finds every crack
every fault the house
screams at its
seams

s t i l l

lost birds in
broken light windows
gone limbs strewn across
debris filled riverbed we called
our street power lines sparking setting
fire to the empty house next door someone's
screaming one block over someone's screaming
someone's screaming no no no no screaming no no
no no one's coming to help us   at least not for days

II.

GHOST FORESTS

Some hauntings are absence:
a name half-remembered,
concrete steps to nowhere
where a house once stood.

Others are just silence pressed into the earth.

08/31/2021 1200 / ORLEANS PARISH

In a little torn blue tent in the Calliope, a young Black woman is curled and shaking on her side, her left arm grotesquely swollen, skin taut and shining. She can't be older than nineteen. When I ask, *do you know where you are right now?* She looks up with glazed eyes and says, *mommy.* I call 911, then again in thirty minutes. Three hours later, in the ambulance light, her arm looks red, mottled.

Two days later, I startle awake from a dream about her arm, the swelling, the discoloration. The way some losses can't be measured.

A BODY IN PUBLIC

On his birthday, the day after mine,
a cold November morning,
Bobby Earl Fowler woke to headlights glaring,
a grainy speaker barking,
Move along!—no compass, no *where*.

Then Christmas night, one month later,
he settled on a park bench by the shelter,
$200 ticket tucked in his shirt pocket
like a wilted boutonnière,
and never rose again.

Death by statute, by ordinance,
by systematic abandonment
disguised as public safety.
I didn't know my birth father.

But I know the deadbolt's
click, the company
of cold concrete, the empty
street's menace, corpus craving heat
like tina, arms eaten alive
on alleyway mattresses.

I know a body's march
til hunger shifts, til the 7-11 mirror
casts a ghost with familiar eyes,
til $3 flip-flops wear a hole clean
under the heel, each step pressing
earth that refuses to claim me.

I traced his steps in arrest reports,
mugshots sagging year by year, on display
in Publix checkout racks, wedged between
Santa Claus Found Frozen in Iceberg
and *Vaccines: The Scandalous Truth*.

Ocala Sarasota
Pensacola Tallahassee

As if motion could save him,
as if he could outpace the laws
labeling his body illegal, as if
he could end the chase, finally
catch a little undisturbed sleep.

What remains when the cot's taken,
when the sentence is another night
outside, when the judge calls you
vagrant, never Vietnam vet?

They took his name, his last dollar,
and flung him back to the pen.

Can a soul trespass in its own skin?
Can a man be illegal in all places
simultaneously?

And when he died on that park bench,
was it still public ground?

Or did his body, at last, belong to no one?

08/31/2021 1900 / ORLEANS PARISH

The elected official's Italian leather shoes weren't made for this place. He should know better, purportedly being from right around here. *Wear boots*, I'd texted. *Closed-toed, thick soles.* He looks doubtfully at the ground as we distribute water bottles and sandwiches. I shouldn't need to tell him about the needles, the broken glass, the things that can puncture more than shoes. His district, but clearly terra incognita. He poses for quick photos, checks his watch. His driver waits with the engine running. I don't know what time it is, only that the sun will go down on our dark city soon, and I've got about 100 more sandwiches to pass out.

VISITING HOURS

The last time I came here, this
bone-bleach square beside Prytania,
I didn't come for ghost stories.

I came to leave a pack of Camels
out front of your family vault and
say farewell to you and this ruin city.

But the gates open to everyone.
Tourists swarm like termites,
and a man in a straw hat calls out,
This is where Lestat turned him!

A pair of women laugh so hard
they knock over a vase of plastic lilies
and don't notice. A father of four
poses on a step like it's Versailles.

I waited for quiet, but it didn't come.
So I crouched low, pressed the pack
below a rust-flaked corner of stone,
palmed the top twice, a gesture, I guess.

A boy pointed at me and asked,
Is he doing voodoo?
and his mother turned red,
turned away, said nothing.

There's no reverence in this kind of heat,
just the reek of tour bus bodies,
the sour rot of beer and piss,
the city smell I think you'd laugh at
if you were still laughing.

But I remember how you lit every room
like a match,
and how quiet the fire was
once it caught.

08/13/2016 0500 / IBERVILLE PARISH

Memory follows no path at all. When I was a child, my first grade teacher told me that water has memory. *That's why holy water works*, she said. Now I wonder: does this water remember being in my lungs? Does it remember the Gulf, the clouds, the levees that couldn't hold it? Does it remember when we let the river chart its own course?

Does it remember my house from before?

RECORDS OF BIENVENUE

Diocese of Baton Rouge Catholic Church Records,
Volume 5, page 592:

> *WAGUESPACK, Bienvenue, age 4 mos.*
> *(Thelesphore & Seraphine LOUPE)*
> *bur. 13 Dec. 1838, at St. James Cemetery*
> *(SMI-4, 135, also SJA-4, 67)*

Four months
in St. James Parish.
Bienvenue. Welcome.
A son named for arrival,
not in anticipation of his departure.

Left undescribed is Seraphine weeping,
Thelesphore's hands digging into marsh
that would not stay open, a feather-light
box, small enough for one man to carry.

> *Add Bienvenue to your family tree.*
> *Click here. Confirm relationship.*
> *Is this your Ancestor?*

The genealogy website can't understand
I collect ghosts who haunt no one but me.

Two centuries later, I lurk in the online
archives. Even the dead migrate away
from paper, shelves, and weeping batture,
into data centers on higher ground.

It's easy enough to imagine that day.
Sugarcane cleared from December fields,
Loupe hands stained from kettle scrapings,
the gauze of molasses steam and river-fog
settled low over St. James Parish.

The archives can't say: if Bienvenue was dressed in white,
if marsh birds sang during the burial,
if Seraphine kissed his cold forehead
one last time before the coffin closed;
if his name was ever spoken at the dinner
table, or if silence became another family
member; if Thelesphore carved a small
wooden cross, and if he wept only
when he knew none could see him, grief
measured differently for fathers then.

Then there is this: *SMI-4, 135, also SJA-4, 67.*

The burial, noted in duplicate.

In 1838, it was decided this child
would not dissolve without witness.

So, for now, I can tell you: A child named Bienvenue lived
for four months in 1838.

The river that flooded his grave
now threatens mine.

08/31/2021 1900 / ORLEANS PARISH

José Andrés's shiny black fleet has commandeered a parking lot. Someone unfolds a city map across a plastic table. *Here*, I say, pointing to spots along the river, beneath the overpass, around the big cathedral. *And here, and here.* My fingertip leaves grease marks on the shiny map—X marks the forgotten. The chef nods, makes notes on his phone. His team loads luxury SUVs outfitted with industrial kitchen equipment, warming trays. I'm surprised by their efficiency and seriousness. The ham and cheese croissant he hands me is the first hot food I've eaten in a week. It's delicious.

POLITICAL THEATRE

Author's Note: *On the evening of Tuesday, March 18, 2025, the State of Louisiana, under the direct orders of Governor Jeff Landry, executed Jessie Hoffman, Jr., age 46. Department of Corrections officials restrained him on the gurney with brown leather straps and secured a plastic gas mask over his face. They forced nitrogen gas into his lungs, suffocating him to death for 19 minutes, witnesses describing his final minutes as violent and full of obvious pain and suffering. Louisiana law prohibits the use of gas to induce hypoxia as a method in the euthanasia of animals.*

This was the first execution in Louisiana in fifteen years. Reporting in The Lens described the rehearsals conducted by prison staff ahead of the 2010 execution of Gerald Bordelon. Molly Fowler wrote, "From our room, we could see only two things. The machine that would push the poison into his veins in three steps. And the feet of the guard playing Bordelon. As I was watching, I saw that he was trembling. . . I had never considered that this process, Gerald Bordelon's execution, might affect him. I had assumed he was in it for the overtime."

ACT I: REHEARSAL

[*Curtain rises on the gurney*]

Closed doors for a closed rehearsal,
learning the choreography of death.
Officers walk their colleague to
the gurney, practiced pallbearers,
the timekeeper counts each step.
The one cast as condemned twitches
as they strap him down, a reflex
that can't split the hands that kill
from the feet that march to orders.

Governor—can I call you Jeff? Tell me,
do you ever watch these dry runs?
Have you seen the stage dressed, the blade
glint, the hungry fire snap at the wood?

ACT II: HISTORICAL PERFORMANCE

[*Shadows sway on the platform*]

Once, in Alexandria, the gallows groaned
under bodies too young, too Black to choose
their governor, planks creaking beneath their
swing, crowds buzzing low like flies.

Once, in Franklin, Camellias rode at night, their
robes once white, but gritty with ash and bone-dust,
hooves soft pattern on the cotton fields' edge,
kerosene sharp in the humid summer air.

Once, in Opelousas, the mob needed three things:
a name, a lie, a cypress to bear the weight.

In this
blood
stained
boot,
a trial's
just a
longer
rope.

ACT III: MODERN PRODUCTION

[*Lights flicker in Angola*]

In Bogalusa, the night riders ride still,
headlights replacing torches, laughter
snapping like sparks over radios,
black boots shining, hands still stained.

The chamber waits, props lined up,
script locked in. Your signature smudges
the air with coal, a mark that coils
Angola's throat. Jeff, do you sleep
through the clank of that gurney rolling?
Nitrogen chokes quiet, you say,
as if a soft death unties the rope's old grip.

And don't we always swear it won't happen again,
then build the same rooms?

Still, your hands don't shake, still, the antiseptic stench
drowns fear's rust blooming under bleach.
Still, the state fills its bank with bones.

EPILOGUE

[*Curtain falls*]

Outside your office, I watch mockingbirds
weave nests from torn-up death warrants,
their wings brushing your name, their songs
clanking like keys, thudding like doors,
choking like last breaths, names called out
louder than you wrote them.

When the spotlight dims, when the seats go cold,
programs balled up in fists, when the silence fades
to a hum that gnaws the quiet for justice
never served—what then, Jeff?

Do you exit stage left and rehearse your next line?
Or does some small piece of you feel the twitch
in your own legs when death walks off the page
and looks us all in the eye?

08/13/2016 1300 / IBERVILLE PARISH

Things that don't float:

the good towels
insurance policies
your mama's rosary
the last frozen deer meat
trust in government agencies
everyone's grandparents' ashes
the dog that wouldn't get in the boat
the certainty that it won't happen again

NOVEL ECOSYSTEM

I.

A boy in Vacherie, 1922, bleeds from the ear.
His crime: a familiar greeting, *bonjou*.
His son seals his lips against his children, a mercy by silence.
The hollow inheritance of empty sound.

What survives when speech means bloodied knees and knuckles,
when tongue is contraband and children learn silence before syntax?
L'anglais ou le bâton—English or the stick—a choice that
is no choice.

Swallow your father's words, feel them churn in stomach acid,
rough syllables scraping your throat, astringent as green persimmons.

Four decades of erasure, mouth by mouth.
Called assimilation but really, it's *transubstantiation:*

your father's speech transformed
into your body's quiet resistance.

In dreams, you speak three languages that you were never taught.

II.

The law says you are this.
Your body says I am more.

They draw borders on maps. *the scratch of the clerk's pen,*
They draw borders on bodies. *cold metal desk against forearms,*
They draw borders across throats. *hum of fluorescent lights, incessant*

Trans beyond any single crossing, a perpetual liminality
that legal systems comprehend only as threat and contradiction.
I stand before the mirror, practice my own taxonomies,
name myself with words they never taught me.

The state demands coherence but offers none in return.

III.

They call it *ghost forest*, but the trees aren't dead,
just learning to drink salt.

The newsman says tragedy.
The scientist says *novel ecosystem.*

What emerges after collapse, neither pristine nor ruined,
a third thing, a survival thing, a perpetual becoming.

Three days after the flood, I find an oak
sapling bolting through my bedroom floor.
The house is compromised, the insurance claim denied.
The contractor says structural damage.
I say *beautiful, terrible life.*

I trace the veins on its leaves, whisper apologies for the foundation,
gratitude for its persistence, awe at our parallel survival.

We carry what matters in our bodies—each cell a floating ark,
each word a seed waiting for ground that does not yet exist.

This morning, I watch grackles weaving nests
in the skeletal arms of the abandoned refinery,
their oil-slick feathers opalescent against the rust,
their calls metallic, relentless,

unquestionably alive.

III.

LAZARUS SONGS

The body wasn't supposed to make it this far.
And yet, *here it is.*

MAYBE YOU SHOULD WRITE A POEM

The Union Pacific—subzero and starved.
Between greased screeches, someone shatters,
then screams. No poets among us, least
far as we knew. No missing posters;
we'd torched them bridges for warmth.

Then there's all y'all always rollin' in,
gap-year North Face nomads, class rebels
with Moleskines penning hermetic highway
memoirs, chokin' on metaphor, looking for soul
in all the wrong places like the railroad
or onramp might could owe revelation.

Publish your curated skid-row zines!
Reap your ovations at Iowa readings!

I'll be here, tracing barb-wire ridges
on tattooed knuckles, no byline, no prize,
no road souvenirs. One pill kicks me up.
Three put me down. No tracks ever spared me
the brand or the scar. No mat for the crash,
no mask for the smoke. Just rust in my mouth
and spit black with tie-dust.

I stole your Black Diamond gloves, your new bandana,
your crushed pack of cloves, and your Adderall.

Maybe you should write a poem about it.
Maybe it'll win a Pushcart.

08/15/2016 0700 / IBERVILLE PARISH

Mold blooms in patterns like sea coral, like topographical maps of countries that don't exist, like the living shadows of Pompeii of everything that used to hang on these walls.

It likes to make a home in your lungs, so I cover my nose and mouth with a red bandana. In seventh grade Louisiana history, we never learned to call our home a resource extraction colony, but we chanted the names of what was pulled from under us: *oil! gas! sulfur! salt!* Now home itself is being extracted, disappearing at a rate of a football field every hour.

COMMUNAL WILL FROM THE LAST DRY-BORN

We leave you scraps salvaged at Mémère's feet,
little fingers grasping at a lost lingua franca,
and in that timeless game of broken telephone,
their legacies become your legends.

We leave you our shunning of the hurricanes,
our refusal of their given names,
how outsiders give themselves away,
saying *Katrina* without flinching.

We leave you the tongue that learned to split in four:
French at the altar, English at the bank,
Kréyòl in the kitchen, silence in the squad car.
If you're much like us, you'll need them all.

We leave you mouth harp songs not written down,
the ones you hum but don't know why,
hambone rhythms holding time,
those front porch open-window blues.

We leave you each other, the bitter cousins
and borrowed aunties, play-kin, god-kin,
friends made in the grocery line. Never forget
you are never alone, and leave no one behind.

We leave you the family bible wrapped in oilcloth—
missing Genesis, intact in Lamentations.

Take the hammer. Take the hymn.
Take the hand reaching out at the dock.

Take the memory of solid ground,

not to return to it,

but to remember what it cost

to leave our footprints underwater.

09/02/2021 2300 / ORLEANS PARISH

Night five of the blackout: I sit dirt-crusted and sweat-sheened on the tailgate of a white pickup. A can of Miller Lite stamps perfect circles on filthy, ammonia-foul jeans, the warm beer a coda to another day spent hauling food, water, and gasoline to every corner of the city.

Suddenly, lights flicker across the darkened blocks of the Vieux Carré. A wave of warm white washes over N. Peters, then Decatur, then Chartres, where I sit. First one building, then another. A collective sound rises—part cheer, part sob—from a thousand windows left open to catch any lazy movement of air. My own voice joins without conscious decision, a joyful, broken, howling from somewhere deep within me.

IN WHICH THE SOUTHERN TRANSSEXUAL POET REFLECTS ON THE PRECARITY OF HIS 20S AS A FORMERLY HOMELESS, PART-TIME CRAIGSLIST SEX WORKER

When the grid failed during The Storm, I re-arranged bowls
across the floor, my archipelago of last chances, drip-drops
from the spigot marking time, each ping an echo of my stut-
stuttering heartbeat.

what
did
I
do
to
survive?

Kept a river rock in my pocket,
worn smooth from worry,
Pressed it against my gums
until they flooded copper,
element recognizing element,
blood acknowledging
stone's ancient patience.

Learned to walk in the smallest
body possible, shoulders curled
forward, eyes down, universal
please-don't-notice-me posture,
the protective hunch of a prey
animal, knowing how quickly
protection becomes predation
in certain places.

Made a temporary home of
my studio apartment
for visiting businessmen;
they slept in my bed,
I slept in my truck outside.
Made a temporary home of
my body for married men;
a temple, yes,
but under renovation,
in need of capital funds.
Whatever it took.
Whatever I could bear.
And many things I couldn't.

The body wasn't supposed to make it. *And yet, here it is.*

THE FIRST JOY

They say the first revels spilled from the storm
tide's pause, cleat-gripping skiffs rung the courthouse
roof. Asphalt shingles clung soft with green, damp
velvet pressed under bare leather soles. Bell
tower gone, the bench sunk, but Spanish moss,
fishbone charms swaying from rafters and eaves.

They say a woman with no tongue, river
stole her words, not her song, sang the first round.
Throat-humming night alive, like what moves and
lives in wave and breath. Flames fanned in rusted
cans, fires fed with names of the dead, stories
rose, not how they left, only how they lived,
quiet hands reaching beyond the tide's trim.

Old man strung a cracked guitar with scrapyard
wire and heirloom screws. Children ran feral,
braiding garlands of eelgrass and grocery
ribbons, small callused hands banged overturned

buckets and the elders began to dance,
old feet tracing older steps in the wet,
newer steps dawning from the last dry-born.

None shed tears besides the river, silver
rise a quiet gift, collecting no toll
in its departure. They danced till the roof
groaned low, a beast unyoked, then danced in the
water's return, ankles trailing algae
like drowned veins, phosphorescence pulsing in
the new-moon dark. Dawn broke with satsuma
skin sting, cypress smoke, alkaline ash tang.

Where salt met fresh, new creatures stirred, a dream
half-remembered but fully becoming.

And when the sun lifted over the drowned
fields, someone said: "Let this be the first joy."

Came the response, "Let it remake us all."

So it's told.

09/03/2021 1500 / ORLEANS PARISH

Smoke from their makeshift grill rises between concrete pillars. Beneath the highway, afternoon light filters through an impossible angle, catching steam from the sausages sizzling on the small charcoal circle. *Stay, eat with us*, they insist, the three of them making space on their sliver of cement. The dad turns the links with a bent fork. The mom tears a single paper towel into napkins for each of us. Their daughter, maybe seven, arranges pebbles in careful patterns beside the grill. I ask what else they need. *Water? Blankets?* The dad looks up with a smile, sudden and bright: *Company*, he says, passing me a hot sausage wrapped in a slice of white bread. Above us, oblivious drivers cross the bridge, going somewhere else entirely.

NOUVO ATLAS LWIZYAN

The old maps lied. Sidewalks where salt licks now bloom,
streets that got swallowed when we were still kids. But,

Collapse births more than a broken before.
And so, we begin again.

The playground on First Street: *Bayou Batay.*
The tilted church steeple: *Our Lady of Crabs.*
The gas station pole sign: *Big Shell Beacon,*
where they light lanterns nightly to guide the boats home.

Where the levee cracked open, we stabbed
plastic forks spray-painted red,
marking the breach as   *Red Tooth River.*

Aunt Ruth never let us rename her street.
She said the water would leave like it always had.
She died still believing it, thank Jesus almighty.
We gave her name to the eastern marsh.

The ferry boat launch where we'd last say goodbye,
we named   *Pointe Adyeu.*

Once we'd finished naming, we made maps of our skin.
I tattooed our trail down my sister's knotted spine:

Gar Graveyard
St. Lucy's Cross
Nouvo Lavil

She says   *If they ever find me, they'll know you're still here.*

TRANSPLANT

I.

I packed lightly: three boxes of books,
a winter coat I'd rarely needed,
two more boxes of books.

Just what fit in a rust-specked Durango,
full of old wasps' nests with a bad
suspension and two working doors.

But my body smuggled contraband:
sweet cane smoke still lodged in lung tissue,
muscle memory of 30 miles of River Road,
my winding commute to Huey's monolith,
two dozen slime green tree frogs clinging
to the hood for dear life the whole way.

II.

I keep my doctor's letterhead, folded in thirds,
tucked inside a manila envelope worn soft
from nervous handling. It's one of many
passports required for crossing invisible borders.

The pharmacist squints up, asks why I need
syringes. I've rehearsed this in every airport
bathroom, at every state line crossing, my body
being contested territory requiring
constant documentation.

The performance of legitimacy, the practiced
and careful modulation of tone—not angry,
not desperate—the practiced smile that says:

I am harmless, I am deserving,
I am prepared for your scrutiny.

III.

I brought a distant ancestor's thick aluminum pot,
now scraping against new burners,
patina darkening with each use.
Northern friends marvel at what emerges,
as if recipes can't survive transplanting,
as if flavor requires a specific latitude,

as if gumbo didn't come here a century ago
on recipes packed neatly in boxes,
tucked carefully in the suitcases of 500,000
seeking liberation, as if my hands wouldn't
remember the moment flour browns
without needing to consult a map.

But the okra I find is woody and long,
picked weeks late by hands that have
never put it raw to their mouths.
I substitute, adapt, use the frozen stuff.

IV.

In winter, my body betrays me,
refuses to acclimate. I shiver at 50 degrees.
Neighbors laugh, say just wait for January.
But it's not just the cold; it's my skin's thirst
and how each breath feels incomplete,
missing its water content.

I slice into a green bell pepper and smell
my uncle's kitchen and geography collapses
and for two breaths, I am on warm white oak,
watching surgeon's hands, large and certain.

Lake Michigan rattles the window,
and I'm back, disoriented by time travel.

My accent thins. Phone calls home bring it
rushing back, vowels stretching like Roman candy.
I speak two languages: *then* and *now*.

V.

I miss the live oak in my yard, branches
sprawling twice as wide as the house was tall.
I miss the bench swing I hung myself, testing
each year whether it would hold a body growing
against its will. I don't miss Lafayette Cemetery
No. 1, where tourists crowd, laughing loudly,

making goodbyes impossible to speak. On my last
visit, I stood in the stone forest breathing in history's
long decay. I still hold now-useless knowledge of which
streets flood first. I know the timing of stay-or-go.
I can find higher ground nearby to park the car.

My survival knowledge is rendered obsolete by latitude.
But my body can't know this. It still braces
for the storm surge during any heavy rain.

VI.

Now there's Lake Michigan, nothing like the Gulf's
warm bath. In summer, it stretches beyond comprehension.
In winter, ice shelves line the shore, bright blue
and sharp-edged architectures larger than cathedrals.
I learn water in new forms: solid, sculptural, patient.

I still don't have the foreign vocabulary of snow:
powder, slush, lake effect, black ice.
But I'm learning the sounds and sensation of salt
crunching underfoot and the way light behaves
differently here, refracting through crystal air,
illuminating buildings that scrape the clouds.

I find queer bars where no one knows me.
Revel in the freedom of selective disclosure.
Rub up against bodies like mine in layers,
gender blurred beneath down and wool.

The streets here are laid out in grid precision,
unlike New Orleans' drunk compass.
They have tornado sirens instead of flood warnings.

I’ve come to love the patient wait for spring,
the way winter burns the eyes
and summer swells with possibility.

New muscle memory forms: the defensive
hunch against a shocking wind. My husband,
Chicago-born, who never knew evacuations
or the dread of watching water rise past doorsteps.
His body carries its own knowledge:

how to shovel snow without straining your back,
which trains run late in February storms,
the timing of salt trucks before dawn.

He teaches me winter survival: layers, not bulk;
wool, not cotton. His hands are steady on my shoulders
as I learn to walk on ice. At night, he listens to my stories
until they become part of him too, his dreams filling
with water he’s never seen.

Migration happens in both directions;
we become each other’s geography.

08/18/2016 1000 / IBERVILLE PARISH

The rental insurance company asks on the phone if I have receipts for items damaged in the flood. I choke on my laugh. Yes, hold on, let me check my waterlogged filing cabinet for the warranty paper on my late grandmother's 7th-grade graduation bracelet.

AUNT MAGNESIA'S CHILDREN

I. Acquisition

On 10 May 1933, they carried torches
to Opernplatz, Berlin's stone heart.
What burned first wasn't Marx
or Lenin or manifestos
of revolution, but the library
of Magnus Hirschfeld's
Institut für Sexualwissenschaft.

Footage from that night shows
young men in uniform, backs bent
under the weight of knowledge,
sweat-shined faces lit by purpose.
They feed twenty thousand volumes
to the pyre. I watch. I taste the
sharp tang of burning glue
and leather, chemical smoke
from developed photographs
curling, blackening, gone.

What I know of Hirschfeld:
his handwriting was precise,
he collected 10,000 questionnaires
on sexual orientation and gender,
developed the modern vaginoplasty,
his patients called him *Aunt Magnesia*,
and he never returned home
to Germany. He died in Nice two
years later, his heart finally giving out.

II. Processing

They designated our bodies degenerate,
each heartbeat adding to a dangerous index.
While books turned to carbon and ash,
Hirschfeld—who'd fled to Paris—watched
newsreel footage from exile, the celluloid
truth of flames consuming his life's work.

Meanwhile at Gestapo headquarters,
officers alphabetize records salvaged
from the institute's metal filing cabinets.
Patient files transition into warrant lists.

III. Deaccession

I think of Opernplatz when lawmakers hold up
printouts of trans healthcare research
from their elevated bench, looking down
as they read selected passages aloud,
stage-lit, surrounded by polished mahogany,
fingers trembling with rehearsed outrage.

I think of burning books when they pass laws
banning my healthcare, when they scrub research
from government websites, when they strike
the word *transgender* from medical guidelines,
when they tell doctors my body is illegal.

Last week in Tallahassee, a clerk
in the Department of Health sits
in a climate-controlled room, backspacing
years of gender-affirming care protocols.

Delete. Delete. Delete.

Cursor blinking like a hand on fire.

IV. Preservation

This is perhaps why we still build
our own archives, tape ourselves saying
this is my voice three months on T, stack
bloodwork results in manila folders next
to referral letters signed by various gatekeepers
who recorded us performing the correct narrative.

This is perhaps why we press photographs
between acid-free pages: *Before. After. During.*
Evidence of survival, evidence of change. We

document each synapse-bright surge
when we recognize ourselves in the mirror,
each moment our bodies become legible to themselves.

My body is an archive they cannot
burn, a book that publishes itself
with every breath, every step.

We are the descendants of ashes, Aunt Magnesia's
children, the embodied evidence that survived
their first deletion. Like wildflowers pushing up
through char burnt fields, we grow in the aftermaths
of their forest fires.

LAZARUS (FRAGMENTS OF PERSISTENT JOY)

The morning after the floodwaters recede,

my neighbor's chickens are loose on our street,
red hens stepping gingerly over debris,
unexpectedly dignified. The elder next door,
Ms. Josephine, calls out from her porch:
They survived! Look at them struuuuuuuttin!
Her voice carries across the mud-slick pavement,
the scent of wet oak and diesel in the air.
Her laughter's so much more valuable
than anything I managed to carry upstairs.

Mid-point of the twelve-hour committee hearing—

my testimony's scheduled for hour nine.
Texts light up my phone: *We're watching.*
You're not alone. Bringing sandwiches at 4.
In the Capitol bathroom during recess,
three of us huddle by the sink,
exhausted from being spectacles, sharing mints
that taste of artificial wintergreen and solidarity.
We look like raccoons, my friend says,
pawing at my face, and our manic giggles
bounce off institutional tile, a sound
they cannot legislate away.

The night forty-seven anti-trans bills

are introduced nationwide,
we project *Paris Is Burning* onto the side
of an abandoned Dollar General,
someone's generator humming along
with the ball scenes. When the cops come,
they just watch for a while, then leave.
Even they can't find the energy to stop this.
Our bodies lean into each other in the dark,
my head on Dee's shoulder, their cologne
like cedar and black pepper.

On screen, Venus Xtravaganza says:
I would like to be a spoiled, rich, white girl.
They get what they want, when they want it.
We've all memorized the line and whisper it
as she says it, our small spell against time.

After the sixth bill hearing,

I come home to find my housemates have built
a throne in our bathroom, ancient alleyway armchair
draped in gold fabric, plastic crown on the seat,
sign reading *YOUR MAJESTY*. The absurdity breaks
something open in my chest. We take turns sitting
on it to pee, royalty in the most contested room
in America, laughing until our ribs ache
with the release of being ridiculous
when they've tried to make us tragic.

In the community garden after the flood,

pulling waterlogged debris from the beds,
Troy finds a tomato plant, somehow alive, tangled
in fence wire carried by the surge. We replant it
in the center plot, christen it *Lazarus*, bring it water
in a procession of mismatched containers. By August,
it produces exactly seven tomatoes, each one shared
between twenty neighbors, sweet-acid burst
against the tongue, the taste of what refuses to die.

The night they passed the ban,

we drink blue liquor at The Levee,
tongues stained like water test strips.
We commandeer the ferry
when Andy's cousin's shift is over,
guitars, camp chairs and empty bottles
of Mad Dog crossing the Mississippi
over and over til dawn. *Closer to Fine*
ping-ponging the battures, our voices
carrying beyond the riverbanks, dogs
in Sunshine and Plaquemine singing along.

On our camelback rooftop during the blackout,

all of South Louisiana is dark except
for occasional generator lights, like lightning bugs.
The heat is unbearable below, but up here,
a breeze. Someone passes a joint, its ember
briefly rivaling Mars. My chest is bare
in the darkness, scars silvered by starlight.
Tomorrow, we'll search for ice, for fuel, for news
of when power returns. Tonight, we find Orion's belt,
steady as ever above our fragile grid, a constellation
of unchanging stars naming nothing about us
but witnessing everything.

04/03/2022 1300 / BALDWIN COUNTY

Seven months past the storm, at a restaurant two states away,
a waiter fills my water glass, and I flinch.

button poetry

NOTES & ACKNOWLEDGMENTS

Thank you to the editors of these journals for publishing the following poems:

Boudin: "Aunt Magnesia's Children" and "Lazarus"

January House Literary Journal: "Subsidence" (nominated for 2026 Pushcart Prize)

The Rumen: "Political Theatre"

Delta Poetry Review: "Communal will from the last dry-born"

ONLY POEMS: "Another Hurricane Poem"

Salvation South: "A Body in Public"

Foglifter: "Tooth Gaps in the Archives," "In which the Southern transsexual poet reflects on the precarity of his 20s as a formerly homeless, part-time Craigslist sex worker," and "Novel Ecosystem"

Thank you to Nicole Stockburger for your brilliant developmental and line editing of one of the earliest versions of this collection.

Thank you to Bryan Borland for being one of its first cheerleaders.

Thank you to Desireé Dallagiacomo and to all my Undercurrent Writing Workshop friends for making the place where so many of these poems started.

Thank you to Tucker Barry, Rachel Berard, and Ira Gerber for being my family.

ABOUT THE AUTHOR

Francis Dylan Waguespack (he/they) is a visual artist, poet, and author of *Tooth Gaps in the Archives* (Button Poetry, 2026), winner of the Button Poetry First Book Award. He makes art about the politics of disasters and being from a place and in a body that both live under threat. His written work appears in many publications including *ONLY POEMS DAILY*, *wildness journal*, *The Penn Review*, and *Foglifter*. He is also a life-long political operative and nonprofit leader working toward LGBTQ+ liberation and housing justice. Find him online at www.francisdylanwaguespack.com.

OTHER BOOKS BY BUTTON POETRY

If you enjoyed this book, please consider checking out some of our others, below. Readers like you allow us to keep broadcasting and publishing. Thank you!

Gigi Bella, *without the frills*
Buddy Wakefield, *Stunt Water*
Ollie Schminkey, *Don't be Afraid to be Bad*
Carson Wolfe, *Coin Laundry at Midnight*
Adrienne Novy, *good luck in the real world*
Rachel Camacho, *Pink Elephant*
Aly Acevedo, *My Dear Cult Leader*
Kristina Percy, *Both True*
FreeQuency, *(On |Un-)Becoming*
Hailey Tran, *an everyday occurrence*
Mickie Kennedy, *Glandscapes*
Chelsea Guevara, *Cipota*
Daniel Elias Galicia, *Still Desert*
Jared Singer, *Forgotten Necessities*
Meg Ford, *Wild/Hurt*
Jalen Eutsey, *Bubble Gum Stadium*
Najya Williams, *on a date with disappointment*
L.E. Bowman, *Shapeshifter*
Ebony Stewart, *Wash*
Phil SaintDenisSanchez, *before & after our bodies*
Josh Tvrdy, *Smut Psalm*
Neil Hilborn, *About Time*
Eric Sirota, *The Rent Eats First*
Zach Goldberg, *I'd Rather Be Destroyed*
Topaz Winters, *Portrait of my Body as a Crime I'm Still Committing*
Zach Goldberg, *I'd Rather Be Destroyed*

Available at buttonpoetry.com/shop and more!

BUTTON POETRY BEST SELLERS